SIS

YOU GOT THIS

by

CRYSTAL THOMAS

Copyright © 2019 Crystal Thomas

All rights reserved. No portion of this book may be reproduced in any form without permission from the publisher, except as permitted by U.S. copyright law. For permissions request write to the publisher addressed "Attention Permission Coordinator"

authorcrystalthomas@gmail.com

ISBN: 978-0-578-54498-4

Ordering Information: *For information about special discounts available for bulk purchases, sales promotions, fund-raising and educational needs, contact the Author at the above email.*

DEDICATION

I dedicate this book to my mother, Diane C. Veney

Mom I wish you could be here to share with me all that I've accomplished. I want you to know that if it was not for you I would not be who I am today. You asked me to leave a legacy mom and that's my goal. You've instilled in me to be a leader and that is what i will continue to do. Watch my accomplishments and continue to keep me covered.

I Love & Miss You Dearly.

THANK YOU!

God,

for stripping me to the core so I could recognize that I am nothing without you. Thanks for showing me that everything I am is because of your grace & mercy.

Khalief & Bashir (Sons)

for putting up with my ups and downs along with my attitude. I love you guys to no end y'all both are a huge part of the reason I motivate myself to do more in life. Always remember to lead by example.

Autumn & Kodi

I love you two so much words could never describe the joy you both bring me. I promise to always be the best Grandma too you both.

Darlene & Tyniesha

Sisters; I love y'all and will continue to be a role model for y'all! I want the best for y'all. Thanks for y'all patience and understanding!!!

Friends

It's way to many of you to name individually but y'all know exactly who y'all are! Thanks for never leaving my side; I owe you guys. Thanks for always telling me when I was wrong. Thanks for being there when I needed to talk, scream, cry, or get out of the house. Love y'all.

Odessa

Thank you Boo; it's only been 7 months and it feels like much longer. You are an amazing woman with such great talents. You pushed me to be a writer while amazing me with your writing talent. I hated to read but eventually it grew on me with your push I finally developed more patience with reading. You showed me that it was possible for me to be an Author every time I doubted myself. Thank you for your commitment to my journey and for keeping me focus until the job was complete.

INTRODUCTION

When people say that I'm bitter, I respond; "No I'm better"! Something happened to me that I never saw coming. Angry! Hurt! Devastated! Confused!

Yes, I was all of that. I knew that I had not done anything directly that deserved the level of betrayal that I've experienced. Was I perfect? No, Yet I did not expect to ever be where I am today. I really didn't see it coming. Yet here I am. I prayed and asked God countless times to carry me through this storm. Thankfully, he did. I am proud of the woman I am today. Yet, through many days I have had to look at the woman standing before me and learn to love and accept myself.

I am enough!

I had to rebuild my confidence. Now, when I look at the reflection staring back at me, I can stand confidently and boldly and proudly say; Sis You Got This!

I started loving myself and truly living. I had no other option. I discovered that I had spent 32 years of my life being the best mom I knew how to be, and 23 years being the best wife I could be. I had neglected to take care of myself. Other than being a mother and a wife, I didn't know who I was. How could such a thing have happened?

I was so focused on being everything to everybody else that I was nothing to myself.

I thank God over and over again for forgiving me. I put a man's happiness and well-being before God. I'm thankful that I can now clearly see my wrong doing. I started discovering things that I liked to do and did them. I started spoiling myself not with materialistic things but with the knowledge of knowing my self-worth. I started planning things that I loved to do. I actually found me!

And for that I have to say "Thank you Lord".

What I did not do is love me first. I encourage whoever is reading this book to never be afraid to face your fears and get out of your own way. You have to learn to embrace yourself. There are always people you can talk to. So, don't ever feel alone. Seek help for the things that have happened in your past that may be hindering your growth and healing; TODAY!

I pray every woman reading this book knows that there is light at the end of the tunnel. You can step out on faith and trust God to guide you.

When you look in the mirror, I want you to know that the reflection you see is just the cover of your life story. Once you realize that it's just a reflection of your stories, you can turn the page to reveal the next chapter of your life. I am speaking to the broken women who has struggled with putting herself back together. I am speaking to the woman who was once me.

THE BEGINNING

CHAPTER 1
CHILDHOOD

Growing up was fun from what I can recall from my childhood. My sister Sharon, and my cousins who felt more like brothers; Tony, Shawn, and I were raised in the same household. We lived in a big 3-story home on Union Street in Philadelphia. My family was a big one. After my grandmother passed away at the very young age of 43. My mom being the oldest took over the household. My mom was the most responsible of my grandmother's seven children. Eventually my mom got her own home, which was much smaller, for just me and my siblings. This was short lived because my aunt and her children soon came to live with us as well as my uncle. We shared so many good memories within the walls of our new home. My mom had a three-bedroom home on the 3800 block of Mt Vernon St, but she made room for our additional guests. We were a family! I remember how creative my mom was when I was growing up. My mom was a great person no matter what role she took on and she was an awesome cook. My mom used to make Easter clothes for my sister, our neighbor Danielle, and myself. We used to go to dance class and we performed in our neighborhood community center for the Christmas holidays. I have so many memories of precious moments that I'll cherish forever. We used to have talent shows and singing contests all the time. Everyone wanted to be Stacy Lattisaw or Tina Marie. My friends, sister and I had dance routines for each hit song and still know them to this day. I can't forget about the quarter parties my mom let us have on weekends. We had some awesome times. There was always something to do in the community and within my neighborhood.

My mom would have card parties and that was her way of making extra money when she did not have to work in the bar. There would be a lot of people at our house, especially men. My mom was known for her good food. Mom always made sure Sharon and I had the latest clothes and the best toys for Christmas. We survived the gang wars back then even though our uncles and their friends were involved. It was a scary time to live through.

INNOCENT AND NOT GUILTY

As much as I try not to remember, I recall my innocence being stolen by men much older than me. During my mom's infamous dinner and card parties I remember two of her close friends making gestures towards my breasts and licking their tongues out at me. They would wait until no one was looking. That was something that I kept from my mom and everyone else. These are some of the things I learned to bury deep down inside of me because I did not want to be labeled as a fast kid. I should have been able to talk about these things to my mom, or another adult that I could trust. At the age of 10 my body had developed much more quickly than my mind. I had a body of a woman but not the maturity. I had no idea that some men preyed on young girls like me.

I can never forget the neighbor that I used to go to the store for would also have me help her do things around her house. I was happy to help out. She was older and that's what I enjoyed doing and still do. A few times when I was helping her out, her son who was six years older than me, lured me into his room by saying he needed me to do something for him. When I went into his room, he asked me to help his friend out who was not feeling well. His friend was his penis. He asked me to kiss it to make him feel better. Not understanding completely, I did it. This led to him forcing me to put my mouth on his penis. I was told to not tell anyone because he would get in trouble. I was very afraid. I made sure to avoid going in his house after that encounter. Some time had passed and I saw him outside one day. He said his mom had been needing help and I hadn't been there. He asked me what was wrong, and I said nothing. I was scared. I finally went back and helped again. This time, he kind of forced me to do it by telling me it helped him feel better. The last and final time, I remember his brother interrupting us with a knock on the door. He made me hide in the closet until his brother went to the bathroom. I felt so ashamed. I did not know what to do. I buried this awful memory deep inside of me. Now, as a woman, I didn't realize the pain I caused myself by burying this memory inside me. I felt worthless, hopeless, lost, ashamed, and less than a person. These feelings grew with me and have had a great impact on my life. In my mind I questioned myself. Who am I? Why am I here?

I was a child, why did this happen to me? All of these unanswered questions that I couldn't answer turned into depression.

All I wanted to do was be a kid. I knew his actions were wrong but could not tell anyone because I thought I was going to be in trouble. I blamed myself. Time passed and I learned not to think of it anymore. I did not want to go into anybody's house again. Yet, that wasn't me. I wanted to be the helpful kid I had been before. I soon started going to the store for my neighbors and helping them out with other things. I wish I had had someone to teach me good touch from bad touch back then.

My mom was well known on the block. I remember as a kid, I wanted to give my mom a surprise party. I talked to a few of my mother's friends who all agreed to help. We all came together and gave her a nice big party. She was so surprised.

On August 14th, my mom turned 28, and 5 days later she had my little sister. We were so happy to have a baby sister. She was fun to have around. For me, having a little sister around and helping raise her was fun; and it became my life. We had some fun times and great memories.

My mom never had a real job; she worked in the neighborhood bars but she made sure home was always taken care of. At the age of 13, things became a whole lot different for us. Our mom, at age 29, was introduced to drugs; and boy was this a hell of an emotional roller coaster!

THE
MIDDLE

CHAPTER 2
SPIRALING DOWN

At 13, I now carried with me the stress of making sure my siblings were taken care of. I didn't even know then what it meant to have no worries and put myself first. My childhood was instantly gone. I was now the leader of my family. Drugs consumed the adults some used them and some sold them. I learned quickly how to be responsible. Soon it became a struggle to manage the house, look after my little sisters and go to school; so, I dropped out.

I was flunking 8th grade. I lied to my mom and let her believe that I was graduating. I wanted her to feel how I felt. She had robbed me of a normal childhood so I would rob her of this moment of pride. My mom couldn't afford to buy me an outfit; so, I borrowed my friend's dress. She had graduated a year prior. I even managed to have my mom curl my hair. I went to school on the day of graduation knowing I would not be walking. This was my call for attention. I wanted my mom back so badly. I'd lost her to the drug addiction. Maybe my mom would see and finally understand that I needed her; we all did. Graduation day didn't play out how I anticipated it. I was hoping my mom would realize that I needed her but she did not seem to care. My mom was very angry. I thought I would embarrass her but I was the one actually embarrassed when my mom called me a "dumbass". I just wanted my mom to see how much we needed her and how much we missed her but that did not happen.

Many days while growing up, I found myself wondering if being dead would be better than my life. Those thoughts were quickly suppressed because my sisters needed me. I couldn't imagine what would have happened to them if I was no longer around. At age 15, I didn't really care about my life. I was doing anything to get by. I soon got pregnant. I was now 15, pregnant and an 8th grade dropout. It definitely wasn't a good look.

My mom was angry at me and I guess she wanted to teach me a lesson. My great uncle gave her money twice for me to get an abortion, and both times she spent it to feed her addiction. WOW! I thought, what did I get myself into? I am pregnant and I was actually going to have to deliver a baby. I was a single teenage mom raising my son alone. My son's father denied his responsibility so everything was on me.

CHAPTER 3
MAJOR STRESSOR

Preparing to become a new mom and trying to figure out how things would work while raising my siblings at the same time was extremely stressful. Back in the 1980s, I remember my son's father's last name began with a W and mine was Veney so our mothers had the same case worker at the welfare office. His mother told the case worker that I was blaming her son for fathering my child and she requested a blood test. She believed her son when he said he wasn't my child's father. His mother believed her son wouldn't lie and he told her he had an STD, so he couldn't possibly be the dad. So, welfare stated that they would pay for the blood test but since his mom requested it, if the blood test came back positive he would have to pay for it. The blood test came back 98.10% that he could not be excluded as the father. He was the father. I still had to raise my son alone because his dad was uncooperative and still said that my son did not belong to him. This journey to single motherhood was about to begin.

So, my journey of being a single mom while still raising my siblings began. I was a young woman who had very little education and very low self-esteem. I was a big girl and didn't feel pretty. I always was teased and couldn't afford what I wanted for myself. I was never motivated, didn't want to go get a job because I didn't have an education and I couldn't complete the Ged in the teenage parenting program. I did attend classes but I just could not grasp the math and reading. I did not ask for help. I was already feeling hopeless so I did not feel I wanted to get help because I just knew that I would not pass. Education was the last thing on my mind. I was worried about finding a stable home for my son. I was clearly not focused.

ADDICTION

The shame of being a child of a drug addict made me very sad. I couldn't go to my mom for help. I blamed her for a lot that was going wrong in my life, because of her addiction. I felt like my mom didn't care about anything. I felt like it was one of the worst moments in my life. My grandmother had 7 children and all were addicted to some sort of drug; be it crack cocaine or heroin. It was crazy to actually live through this. At that time I did not believe I would overcome these stressors or be comfortable talking about it. Being the oldest and having to take on the responsibility for the family, I eventually learned to just deal with it and to care for my family the best I could.

3 of my 5 uncles were alcoholics and drug addicts. They came to live with us when I was growing up so we shared our living space a lot. There were a lot of adults in the house and nothing to eat for us because their addictions came first. From Mom selling her food stamps to making us go borrow money, I remember always feeling embarrassed. I did not enjoy the typical teenage years of fun and carefree living. I was more worried about how we would eat and making sure my sisters and son attended school and daycare daily.

I actually witnessed my mother and a few of her friends sharing a needle to get high, which was heartbreaking. After witnessing this, I recalled going upstairs where my sisters and my son were sleeping and I put a razor to my wrist. I could not mentally process what I had just seen and just wanted to die! This was a lot to handle at 16 years old. My sisters begged me to stop and not to leave them alone. Their pleas woke my son up and he began crying. This was enough for me to get my mind back in the right state. I didn't go through with killing myself, but I cried my heart out that night. I wanted to talk to our mom to help her understand how we felt but she didn't want to listen. She said that she was a grown-up and we should stay in a child's place. Soon I began to steal my Aunt Tracy's food stamps to feed us. This was embarrassing and hurtful because my aunt would do anything and everything for me.

As time went on, I wanted more for my son. I applied for my own welfare check for my son and I to be able to survive. My mom got mad at me. I then called DHS on her. She then put me out on the street with my son so we were homeless. How embarrassing! A homeless young mother and uneducated teenager trying to figure out what to do next. My aunt let us come stay with her for almost a year and a half. I found myself doing things that I thought were a way to get me some extra money.

I began to sell drugs, the money was good but this was not for me. Absolutely not, but I did it to get some money. I sold cocaine for a year or so, but the money I was making started disappearing and somehow the hiding spots that I had were not secret anymore. That's when I realized the addiction in my family was getting real and I had to do something about it. I was wrong for selling drugs. I felt this was the same shit that was killing my family; so, why was I doing it?. I knew I was allowing myself to fall victim to society. After my revelation of how drugs destroyed I stopped and found odd jobs here and there.

CHAPTER 4
TEEN PARENTING

I joined a youth program called *SunnyCrest* to help me with my son. I wanted to be a good mother. While enrolled I met a woman named Joan, who was a social worker. Joan took me and my son in as if we were her own. Joan's guidance is one of the reasons I am the woman I am today. Joan helped me in so many ways to adjust my parenting skills. For that, I'll always love and respect her to the utmost. *SunnyCrest's* focus was on molding us into responsible mothers. I was still making a lot of bad choices. Despite all the assistance and support I received from the program I was still unhappy and fearful of what life had in store for me.

Life was getting a little better and suddenly I got sick. I was expecting another baby and almost lost my life because I didn't know what was going on with me. I thought I had morning sickness. It was, in fact, a blood clot that traveled from my left calf to my right lung. I had to stay in the hospital for 28 days from August 14th until September 11th 1990. It was either my life or the baby. It was a risky pregnancy; something I had to pray about it and let it go. I had a child at home that needed me. I was afraid. I needed as much support as I could get at this point. The doctor informed me that since there were clots in my left lung and in my right calf; this pregnancy was life threatening. It meant I had to make a decision. My life was at risk, so it had to be the baby or me. I had a 2-year old at home so I asked God for forgiveness and terminated the pregnancy.

Life was becoming stressful, raising a child with no education, limited resources and no financial security.

During these times, I once again thought about dying. I would always dismiss that idea when I thought about who would raise my son. I knew I was all he had.

FINDING MY WAY

My living situation was getting worse and I found myself homeless yet again with my son. My friend, with approval from her mother, allowed me and my son to stay for a couple of nights. I was losing hope. I was going from house to house and my depression was growing deeper. I found myself crying more and more. One day, while in class a friend of my mom delivered the good news that I may finally have housing. She informed me that Ms. Peggy had found me an apartment.

Ms. Peggy worked for PHA and did a lot to give back to the community. I was ecstatic; I screamed so loud thanking God for answering my prayers. Finally, a home of my own! I walked in the pouring rain to go and get my keys that day. Now my tears were tears of joy. I got my three big bags and dragged them to my new 2-bedroom PHA apartment. I slept on top of those bags until I was able to afford furniture. I had to wait until my next welfare check. My friend came the same day and gift my son with a bed, food and other household items *(RIP Donnycake)*. This was the ultimate blessing for my son and I.

Welfare and PHA are both temporary programs which I was a part of. I appreciate what the two programs gave me. It was the band-aid to the sore in my life. I began to become stagnated to this life, called the "SYSTEM". I was on welfare living in a Public Housing Authority home and felt life was now good. I didn't have the motivation to do anything but collect a welfare check and live for free. My rent was 19 dollars. I was ok with that because I was not trying to do anything more than just survive. I couldn't see how much I was worth, or all that I truly deserved.

I had always been picked on, told I was fat, teased about my mom being on crack, so I just tried to fit in wherever I went. I didn't focus on how I looked. I made sure that my son was ok and had the latest clothes and sneakers. I walked around with the same jeans on for days with the middle of the jeans worn out. I never cared about my appearance because I was not attractive. I felt like since I was a single mom on welfare, I had nothing going for me, so why care about how I looked. I was hanging in bars, drinking in the casino, gambling and talking to men who sold drugs. I put my son and myself in harm's way several times.

It was nothing but God which kept us safe during those times. My apartment became a hangout. I started selling dinners and having card parties just to have company. I was mimicking my grandmother and mom. I buckled down to the system and became comfortable. My rent was cheap and I received an additional $172 towards my electric and gas bills. This was a good life for me.

CHAPTER 5

INCARCERATION

With no guidance, ambition or dreams I landed in prison. Following behind a friend who was using a stolen credit card, I found myself incarcerated in Montgomery County Prison.

I was 22 years old and scared to death. I had never been in a position where all the rights I thought I had were violated to the max. I had to strip completely naked, squat, cough, and bend over. This was so degrading. I was mortified. I truly committed no crime, but because I walked inside the store with my friend, I was looking at being charged with conspiracy. I vowed not to ever put myself in such a situation again if I got out. I called my mother who came to my rescue 4 days later. My mom found a way to bail me out.

After surviving my prison scare sadly I still continued to place myself in crazy situations. I found out my mom received the money from a male friend of hers. I decided I would repay him. My repayment was sex. He didn't ask but I offered. Soon after, we had a short affair. This man was 20 years my senior. My self-worth was so low that I used sex as a form of repayment. I felt ashamed, so I kept the affair a secret. I felt like this man had saved my life. He did not have to do what he did for me, but he did. I enjoyed our affair but it was short lived. I learned a valuable lesson about how easy it was to get into trouble but how hard it could be to get yourself out.

A NEW START

On August 6th 1994, I met a young man that was interested in me just as much as I was interested in him. My new relationship motivated me to do a lot of things I never thought I could do. In 1995, I enrolled in a CNA (Certified Nursing Assistant) program because growing up; I always said I wanted to be a nurse. So, I had to start somewhere. I completed the program in 6 months and then became pregnant with my second child. After I had my son in 1996, I started working with mentally disabled clients. Then, in March 1997 I moved into a house where my rent was now one dollar, and boy, was I happy.

This time the goal was to go back to school to get my diploma. So, I did some research on obtaining my diploma. Benjamin Franklin Highschool was offering a night program which totally worked out for me. I was able to juggle work, being a mom, going to class, running a household and maintaining a relationship. I only needed a few credits so I only went for one year. I shared that information with all my friends that I knew who did not have a diploma either.

I wanted my children and my other half to see that I could overcome some of the adversities that I had experienced while growing up. In June 1998, I graduated with my diploma and I was astonished. In 1999 I started working as a medical assistant making some money. It was now enough to start the process to get out of the SYSTEM. I was still receiving welfare benefits and insurance until I found a permanent and stable job because I was working for a staffing agency. I do not understand why I just did not do this a long time ago. We had a beautiful home and I appreciated all that the SYSTEM had to offer me but it was time to move on.

All I wanted was to build a strong relationship with my children and boyfriend. I wanted to let them know that if you put your mind to something, it can be done with a little effort. As time passed, we started to become closer. People admired us as a couple. As far as family and friends went, we were always the ones people would come to for advice and support, to the point we started to neglect taking care of our own issues that we were having also. No relationship is perfect, but we made it work. To maintain the relationship I had, I always gave 100 percent and more, when it came to what my other half wanted, not what I wanted. This was a serious issue that I did not see brewing. Now by this time, I was finally ready to buy a house because I had a job. I was not quite where I wanted to be financially, but I was determined. I was focused on moving forward because my children were watching.

Now with two jobs I knew I was ready to get out of the System. I felt like I could finally achieve that goal. I knew my boyfriend wouldn't agree so I fabricated a story. I said that with my income and two jobs our rent was about to increase so we should buy a house. I also did this because the housing authority don't want any one that is not on your lease living with you. They can pop up for an inspection whenever they feel like. If I did not make this move, I would have failed to achieve one of my biggest goals. I stated that we were going to pay the amount of us owning our own home. He eventually agreed to it but he hadn't working a full year yet. So, I applied for the first-time home buyers' program and got a $55,000 loan to buy a home. I included him in my every move but he wanted me to do all the work, so I did. When it came to looking at houses it was always myself and the boys. He was never available but always had so much to say. I figured it's what I wanted for us, so I had to take the lead. I did everything that needed to be done when it came to the household.

CHAPTER 6

BREAKING OUT OF THE SYSTEM

I had a vision and vowed to make it come to life. I went to a first-time home buyer's program where they helped me with my credit. Within months I was able to start looking for a house to buy. My sons and I went to see several houses. It was one hell of a feeling, looking at homes that we might be able to call our own. We looked at 4 to 5 houses and found one we could live in and be happy. On July 19th 2002, I went to the table to purchase our home. It was not that big but it was ours. With minor fixes it was a great buy. I went to return my keys to the housing authority and thanked them for helping me when I needed a home to provide for my children and myself. My manager said she had been working there for almost 40 years and had never seen someone come in and say thank you and she commended me. That was a great feeling. We were now in a home where we could raise a family and set some goals. I was looking for better employment. 4 months after moving in I started applying to new jobs.

Let me break the system down for you in my own words.

At age of 17 I started receiving welfare for my son and myself. When you're in the system you're only a number. It's their way of keeping track of us! We get caught up and labeled as welfare recipients living in the low-income housing. For some people like myself, it's the norm. We hide from real employment because we want to keep paying as little for rent and bills as possible. One day I realized that I could do better and I wanted better. I decided that I wanted to buy a house that I could call my own and in stable employment. I would no longer be, what I feel, is a tracking device in the SYSTEM. I had people say "Girl, stay in there. You cannot beat that rent girl, keep that house. You can alter your paystubs. You can beat the system". I don't think living in PHA or Section 8 is a bad thing at all nor is receiving welfare benefits. These people pry into your entire life and I for one, did not like it at all. They were coming into my home for inspections and wanting my life history. I just wanted more for myself and children. Funny how it took me being in a relationship to realize this.

I finally got an interview as a drug and alcohol tech at the Kirkbride Center. I got hired on the spot with the offer of being a lead tech with maximum pay. I worked there and also kept my part time job in the mental health field. Working in Drug & Alcohol and Mental

Health opened my eyes to why people use drugs and the whole mental health world. I understood what my family was possibly going through. I discovered the various reasons why people said they use drugs, and the reasons why they were depressed and shut down.

I learned about my family history with my grandfather; I began to think that was the reason they turned to drugs. I just could not wrap my head around what I was told about my grandfather and one of my uncles. I always wanted to know why my mom turned to drugs and stopped being the mom we knew, that cared about our well-being and made sure we had what we needed. I kept striving for more and wanted a job with benefits to carry my family and me. In January 2007, I started working at Presbyterian hospital in detox and psych. The only thing, it was the night shift. Yes, it was a change, but I had to realize that change is constant. It was something I wanted so, I did it.

CHAPTER 7
MARRIAGE

Life was progressing and I was truly happy; at least on the surface level. Marriage was something I never thought I would have. Being with the same partner for so long and raising our children marriage became something I started to fantasize about. I felt like we did everything as if we were married; so why not? For years I was wondering if it would ever happen. I felt like I knew this man inside out. Nothing could come between us, so why not get married? I remember carrying the family financially for a while. I was able to maintain everything. After 12 years of being together, my partner proposed to me on May 8th 2005. It was a moment to remember and later laugh about. He knew me and really surprised me. Planning the wedding was an amazing thing. I spent a little less than $10.000 and got almost $8000 back in cash and a paid honeymoon. I had plenty of help from my friends. My mom paid for our pictures to be done *(RIP MOM)*. She wanted to make sure that she participated in something and I was ever so grateful for that. August 6th 2006 was our wedding date. I choose that date because on that day 12 years before, we initially started dating. I can remember that date vividly because I was giving my baby sister her 1st Birthday party. I made spaghetti. My neighbor and James came down the street to get some food. I took his chain from around his neck and told him I was going to be his girlfriend. Ever since that day, we were together and created so many memories. I was still dealing with family issues but he stayed by my side.

My house used to be a meeting place for everyone. Family came and lived with me, stole from me but I knew that would have to end. This was an emotional rollercoaster but I would not trade in the ride for the world. It was well worth the experience. I grew so much and was able to withstand it all.

Marriage is something that is so special and vows should be taken seriously. After 12 years of being together, it was such a beautiful experience because I thought this day would never come. Boy, was I excited! I thought *"I've got to plan a wedding"*! *"Oh, this is like a dream come true."*

We went to marriage counseling. This was when I started to think and I felt like maybe we weren't equally yoked. We both came from different religious backgrounds. James was Muslim and I was Christian. During our counseling session, we were asked *"Will there be any problems because we come from two religious backgrounds"?* I felt like we both loved each other and we shouldn't have any problems with this next step in our lives.

On August 6, 2006 we became one. We were young and married. We enjoyed everything about our wedding; about our marriage and about raising our family. My mom, my grandmother, and my sister all became ill at the time of my wedding, however they all were able to attend. I was happy to see them enjoy and share that memory with them. No marriage is perfect; but you grow through things. What looks good on the outside is not always good on the inside. Trust me. I blamed myself for the things that happened next in my life.

At the end of 2006 and the beginning of 2007, I encouraged my husband to engage more at work and try to get a promotion or at least join a committee. Jobs look at employees' involvements and it's something to add to your resumé. Well, he did. I was so excited that my husband was making an effort to be a better employee. I believed I was being supportive and honestly trying to get my husband to come out of his shell. Then something happened that I could not have seen coming. But it did, and I blamed myself for it. It was something that caught my husband's attention and it was very painful to deal with, especially knowing I convinced him to engage in employee opportunities. That something was INFIDELITY.

I had to go through counseling to try to get an understanding of what had happened, and why. I even checked myself into a crisis center to get some help because my mind was racing. I could not control how I was feeling at all. I became obsessed with things which made my anxiety run high like checking for unknown phone numbers, or certain female comments on social media and his text messages. Trying to return to a normal life was not an easy task. Trying to prove to the world we were this role model as a married couple was not easy. I was quietly breaking down and felt ugly. I felt I needed to compete. I looked in the mirror to find all my faults. I began to blame myself by telling him to be more involved at work and to join those different committees maybe I pushed him into the arms of another woman.

I suffered within myself and wouldn't let it go. I didn't know how I would get past these feelings. It was a struggle. I drove myself into a deep depression. I began to believe that the gifts and trips were something to take my mind off of what had happened. I masked it well. But I believed even more now that all I needed was to do everything and be everything to my husband. As long as he was happy, I was ok. My low self-esteem issues kicked back in and there was nothing that could stop it.

I made this man my God and putting him before God was the worst thing that I did. I would tell people constantly if it was not for my husband I would not have gone back to school, got a job, built a family, paid bills, or had what appeared to be a normal life. When all the while he may have been the motivation for me to get up and get a job, take up a trade to make a career for myself, to be the best mom, wife, friend, daughter, homeowner but it was me who did the work.

ACCEPTANCE

Acceptance is a huge growing part for myself. I've accepted that a lot has happened and I was able to overcome it all. On March 26th 2015, I was admitted to the hospital. The doctors couldn't figure out what was going on with me. To make a long story short; the IVC filter that was placed in me on September 10th 2008 broke and pierced my heart and entered my lung. It was the scariest ride ever. I had to then accept having to be on another blood thinner for my heart indefinitely now. I wanted to live; so, medication for the rest of my life it was. As you read earlier, I had two blood clots in both of my lungs (Pulmonary Embolism) and two blood clots in both legs (Deep vein thrombosis). After many episodes I had to get a medical device that prevent blood clots from traveling (IVC filter) was the medical name for it. It was shaped like an umbrella without a cover over it. This was to ensure that the clots did not travel anymore.

The one I had placed inside of me was recalled 4 months later. I was never notified and it nearly cost me my life. I still have to live with a fragment inside of my lung behind my left breast. I am lucky and humble to be able to stand before you today and say I have not had any further complication. I can't say one cannot occur, but for now, it is contained. You cannot possibly begin to imagine how scary it is to live with something foreign in your body that can move at any given time. I give it all to God because my anxiety was running too high.

While I learned to deal with this foreign object inside my body, I also had to discover that another foreign object had entered my marriage once again. **INFIDELITY!**

THE END

CHAPTER 8
ENDING MY MARRIAGE

On July 1st 2017, my husband decided to leave his family. He said he wasn't happy, that he needed to find himself, and most of all I didn't help him grow as a man. That was a lot to digest and take in. We had renewed our vows 9 months prior. During this time my mom passed away followed by my nephew; now, 2 months later my husband wanted to leave!!!!

In this storm I was going through I had no other choice but to seek God. This couldn't really be happening. I decided to reach out to friends who are married which apparently was the wrong thing to do; I got scolded by my husband. Even with me knowing that he left for someone else and lied to my face about it; I still wanted my husband. I still wanted my marriage that's what I was used to. I begged him to go to counseling, but he refused. I asked if we could date again. I even said that I would forget what happened so we could start over. I did everything to try and save our marriage but I was fighting alone. It was heartbreaking but I tried to maintain my sanity. I was tearing myself down wondering what people thought of me. I began going to counseling alone to try to deal with grief & loss over my marriage. Once again my mental stability took a hit.

We did start dating again. I felt a little hope. I needed to do something. I just couldn't let this man go away just like that. I began to feel like the only one in the boxing ring fighting alone for our marriage. Dating didn't feel the same. It seemed as if he was ashamed of me. I felt dumb, ugly, fat and unattractive. After all of those years, I couldn't have a conversation with the love of my life. I couldn't go out with him around his friends which were both of our friends at one point and time. Ultimately some friends said he asked them to choose between us. And some chose. I still tried to maintain my sanity but then I get a text stating that I was going to have to pay my bills by myself because he was not going to continue to pay where he doesn't live. Wow, 23 years of us having a 2-income household to just one and there were no regards at all. My eldest son asked me when everything first happened *"Mom, do you think he lost you or you lost him?"* He told me to think before I answered. I thought and responded *"Son, he lost me!"*

Almost 2 years went by and I began to talk to God more, humble myself and pray a lot. The man I knew and loved for 23 years was gone. It was a very hard decision to make when I took my ring off in January 2018. It felt like I was throwing in the towel. Months went by and I started making things happen in my life and traveling again. I said I can do this and it actually felt great to start finding me and I loved the feeling. Ending an era is what I now call it. I have now embarked on some new endeavors that have brought me so much joy. Moving on was bittersweet. I still hurt thinking about what was built in our relationship and marriage, but I know the pain doesn't completely go away overnight. It truly doesn't.

Sometimes things that grow together grow apart. Like a beautiful flower if you water it and take care of it the flower will continue to grow. Love it, water it, and nurture it and it will continue blooming. I believed that we had that right at one time. But listen, as time goes by you start to forget that flower ever needed attention. So, it starts to dry and eventually start losing its petals, and slowly withers and dies. Hmmm, pretty much like my marriage. I believe that happened in our case!!!!

Even though it was difficult to accept, and too much at one time to take in. Our relationship became that flower and the love got lost.

Everytime I think about turning back the hands of time; or wishing for a different ending; I remember the flower. And think, Oh no! I can see the roots of the relationship now. The roots are dead and I now see clearly that they can't be rooted again. I learned to talk to God more and friends less! My elevation called for that separation and damn I'm feeling good. I took my life to another level and buried the pass with a shovel!

The grass withers, the flower fades, but the word of our God will stand forever.
(Isaiah 40:0)

He comes out like a flower and withers; he flees like a shadow and continues not. *(Job 14:2)*

REBIRTHED

VALIDATION

There's something about this word that hindered me in many ways. I had the willpower to get up and do a lot of things, but if it might not be approved of, I would second-guess myself and not do it. I always had great ideas. I wanted to do so many things; but I had to ask someone if they approved or agreed with me. If they didn't, I wouldn't do it. That was with clothes, hair, food, drinks and everything else. I felt like I couldn't think for myself, but I always truly knew what I wanted for myself. So, for me, validation means:

Very

Accurate

Loving

Individual

Determined

Accomplished

Tremendously

Impressive

Outstanding

Nurture

CHAPTER 9

BREAKING THE GENERATIONAL CURSE

We have too many women who are suffering within. I want to break the silence. Breaking generational curses is something I vowed to do. I accomplished breaking the generational curse for my family. So, don't ever say that it can't be done. My grandmother had my mom at age 16, my mother had me at 16, and I had my son at 16. All three of us dropped out of school. We all were on welfare and lived in low-income housing. My grandmother was married, my mother never married but I did get married.

My grandmother raised her children alone. My mom raised her family alone. I also was a single mother raising my son alone. I had to maintain and keep my sanity, just to raise my siblings and my son. My grandmother and mom also helped raise their siblings. I wanted better for my son then I had for myself. I didn't take chances with his education while raising him.

My grandmother and mother never completed high school. I had decided to go back, just so I could prove that it could be done within my family. Living in housing authority and being on welfare was something that our family got used to. I've vowed to break these curses. My grandmother was a giving person as was my mom. I mirrored this and wanted to make everyone happy but myself. This is where the low self-esteem came from for me. I see that this was also generational.

I wanted to excel as a mother and be a woman of integrity and break all the generational curses that have plagued my family. From not having an education, to being on welfare, to being in an unstable relationship. I excelled at breaking out of all of those things without hesitation. It took a long time for me to get there but I did it. I also wanted to go and earn a college degree and I did. I became the first person in my immediate family to graduate with a college degree. Yes, I got my bachelor's degree in Criminal Justice and Human Services.

I also wanted to own my own business. I wanted something to leave behind for my children and for my grandchildren to cherish. This will also be apart of my legacy. I came to a decision that I wanted to open up a recovery house for women. Women who want to overcome trauma, hurt, anger, or despair that drove them into a state of depression and addiction. I want to assist those who suffer with mental health issues and also provide job readiness training.

I'm living proof. There was drug addiction in my family to the point where we lost a lot of things and even our home. I could've just become accustomed to the system. I didn't want to be stuck that way. I didn't want my kids to be raised that way. I wanted to do better. I wanted to do more so I had to explore my options and take the test; the test of life. There's a lot of things in life that we miss out on because we do not speak up. We don't want to let anyone know what's going on with us. We should know that one word, one glimmer of hope, one smile or even lending an ear can just lift us in mind and in spirit.

UNHEALTHY MINDSET

For a long time, if things were not sad and happening in my life, I was not happy. That became the attention I looked for. That was not a good place to be. I was content with always being sad and wanted people to feel sorry for me. Do you know how they say that there is light at the end of the tunnel? Well, believe it. I was in that tunnel for what seems like forever. It was not until I opened up and broadened my horizons to venture out and see the world and what it has to offer that I escaped that tunnel. It was a damn good feeling, I must say. I did not see my breakthrough until I was actually broken down. Even though I did not have much of a childhood, I am now beginning to find myself.

I let a lot of the major things that weighed on me heavily this past year go. I stopped playing the victim so instead of asking, why me; I learned to ask, "Well why not you, Crystal?" I willing stayed in a position that had to end. Once I stopped taking on the victim role I finally discovered that I deserve more. God showed me a new path and I now trust him and follow his lead. I now know that nothing could ever get in my way again and stunt my growth.

In October 2017, I started taking Zumba classes and walking St. Joe's track to get some relief from the amount of stress that I was under. Walking turned into working out. It felt great to actually know I was doing something that I enjoyed myself. I actually looked forward to it each week. The walking led to the inches being shed off. With Zumba, I stayed at the back of the class. I was still ashamed to look at myself in the mirror which was in front of the class, I was embarrassed for people to see me trying to do the moves the instructor was teaching. I was discouraged because I did not catch on to the moves right away. Eventually, I got it but I was still not ready for the front of the class, or even to look into the mirror at myself. Than someone introduced me to a twerk class.

Tuesday became my favorite day of the week; Twerk Tuesday I called it. So, from October 2017 to April 2018, I lost not only inches but pounds were leaving too. Yes, THANK GOD, and I was not even trying to lose weight. It just happened. I'm not complaining. The timing of this was amazing. I began to post pictures of me while at the track and while at class. People began to comment which was encouraging for me. A few people came and joined me in class. What I saw as just sharing information turned into *"Crystal you truly inspire me"*. I started to share the things I was doing to make me happy and discovered a lot of people are carrying heavy burdens. I dropped so much weight; that was much needed. Yesssssss! DEAD WEIGHT! I went from a 20 to a 16/18. Dropping the weight made me feel good; finally I did something for me.

CHAPTER 10

GROWTH

For me Growth was about:

GLOWING

RECOGNIZING

OWNING IT

THRIVING

HONORED

October 2017 my mind started shifting to the future I said

STOP BLOCKING YOUR BLESSINGS & START BLOCKING BULL SHIT!!!!!!

I started a new set of goals! I would learn how to drive, get a new job, get into fashion, attend graduate school, and end my marriage.

LEARNING TO DRIVE

October 2017 I wanted to gain my independence. So, I took a leap of faith. I took the permit test 3 times before I passed!!! I really cried tears of joy, not believing that it was real. I passed the permit test but then reality hit (I had to drive now). I prayed! I was ready to be free from all the things that I grew dependent on others to do for me. The fear had to go away. I scheduled driving lessons with Nigels Driving School, December 30th 2017. After my driving lessons I had to schedule my test for my driver's license. I looked at the schedule that they had available and one stood out to me. It was Valentine's Day I thought "love yourself, love what you are doing and most of all conqueror what you set out to do!"

February 14th came and I was nervous as I possibly could be. Despite my nerves I passed my driving test. Thanks to my willingness, and determination, I was finally gaining some independence. A few weeks later, on March 8th 2018, I bought a car. I can't believe I actually was able to do this without second guessing myself or getting approval first.

NEW EMPLOYMENT

I was put in a difficult situation at work but wasn't doing anything about it. I was comfortable with what I was doing. I was a unit secretary with a bachelor's degree. I had the job for two years and wasn't attempting to find employment in the field I wanted. I wanted to work with women in recovery, along with opening my own program eventually. I started applying to jobs in the career I wanted. I applied for a job as a case manager for homeless women. I applied on July 4th. On July 12th I was offered the position. Wow! In the span of 1 week, I applied, interviewed, and hired. This came at the perfect time. I knew it was God directing me to something better. I couldn't thank God enough.

FASHION

I felt like I needed a change to make myself look and feel good about myself. Since I started to discover myself; I needed to look like I wanted to feel. In the midst of my marriage falling apart I almost lost myself. So, I took small steps to start discovering me. I began to dress differently, I felt better and slowly, but surely shifted my focus solely on me. Looking in the mirror to fix my hair or brush my teeth was all I did. I never really looked to see me. I never saw how stunning and gorgeous I was until 7/13/18. I was invited to a party and the week leading up to the party. I had a nice dress and I needed to accessorize the dress. I went to Nordstrom rack to find something that would look appropriate.

On the night of the party, I got dressed and found the perfect jewelry, belts, and shoes to put on with the dress. It was absolutely a sight to see when I looked in my full-size mirror. I looked at myself for the first time ever as a beautiful woman. I finally started to believe this. I began motivating myself to just admire what I see before my eyes. Then it began to be all about me and all that I was capable of. I wanted to inspire myself and others. I wanted to get to know myself and focus on the things that bring me joy.

I had a women's empowerment group to introduce my future business (recovery house). Everyone started complimenting me on how I dressed and accessorize my outfit. One day a good friend of mine introduced me to the woman who got me started with plus size modeling.

Modeling class was fun. I met four women while modeling. I expressed to them my desire to be a fashion stylist more than a runway model and they encouraged me. Modeling seemed like a wonderful idea to help me reach my goal in fashion. I did not have a clue about modeling or walking in heels. Well, I figured that would be where I would start.

I met my model coach through a great friend of the family. Prior to me meeting her and starting class, I spoke with her often over the phone. We shared some of the same ideas also. I told her a lot about me and what I was going through. We laughed, we cried and we shared some ideas. Model class was $25.00 dollars per month. I was coming out of my shell more. We had fun through learning the basics of walking, and I looked forward to practice 2 times a month. We did photoshoots as well as modeling clothes and hats for small boutiques. The coach had her favorites when the class began and it was ok because these women had been with her modeling for some time. I would accept that for now.

But in November 2018, a boutique owner wanted some models and we needed our bags and to wear our signature shirt. I arrived ready to model. I did not realize that I was the problem until the coach told me that I needed big shirts to cover all of my ass. She was supposed to empower us; not make us feel unpretty or discouraged. The coach knew I was battling with low self-esteem and didn't care what came out of her mouth. I learned that this woman had hidden agendas. Instead of feeling sorry for myself and taking on my victim role I stopped modeling and learned a very valuable lesson; watch who you let pray for you because they can actually be preying on your downfall.

I started shopping and making very inexpensive purchases making it look like I'd spent a lot of money. I am a very thrifty shopper when it comes to clothes and shoes. I was once the one who did not like the way I looked in photos. I didn't like my smile because I had 2 teeth missing. I refused to smile and show teeth. I would spend money on unnecessary things and not even for myself. I applied for care credit and was approved. So, I got two implants to replace the missing teeth. So, now when I smile it's still not as beautiful as I want it; but I'm working on it. Going to photo shoots and posing for pictures made me confident and bold. I am showing my curves more than ever. I am trying to encourage and inspire big bold and beautiful women of all ages. It took me a long time to see that I have what it takes to inspire people. I didn't realize it before because I was too busy worrying about everything else but what was important; me!

REBUILDING

CHAPTER 11
GRIEF AND LOSS

I want to take the time to pay tribute to my mother!!!! My mother is the only reason I became who I am today. I want to say "Thanks mom, you were tough on me, but I thank you for that. My, you angered me a lot and I again thank you for that. Mom you were the key to the family and you were suffering inside. Mom, I love you. I miss you. No one can ever take your place. Thank you for teaching me the importance of family and showing me love.

In October 2016, my mom died. Speaking with the hospice care case manager helped my sisters and I understand and accept that the end was near. But I can tell you, September 25th 2016 will always be a day I remember. My mom called me, crying uncontrollably. Her exact words were "*They do not know what they are talking about*". My mom promised me not to tell my family. As heartbreaking as it was to withhold this painful information I respected her wishes.

On Monday, my mom did not show up for dialysis. I called her friend Vicky whom she stayed with. She said my mom was asleep. Vicky wanted her to rest and I said ok. Tuesday came and I called my mom and discovered she was in the hospital. I went directly to the hospital to find my mom lying in a fetal position in extreme pain. I no longer could keep her secret. I called everyone that I was supposed to call; sisters, grandkids and her siblings. It was very hard to explain to them what my mother had disclosed to me 2 days before. Wednesday came and Mom was able to request who she wanted to see and the foods that she wanted; and we made it happen. She wanted greens, potato salad, fried chicken, and pigs' feet.

Well, that was 2 days without dialysis. Her stomach was filled with fluid and infection. The doctors wanted to do a bedside tap to her stomach to release the fluid. That evening my cousins and all my mom's friends came to visit her. It seemed as if she had a burst of energy from somewhere. She was singing and trying to sit up to dance. That was a day filled with laughter and happiness. Thursday came and as the doctors prepare to remove the fluid, my sisters and I had to meet with the case manager from hospice care. The case manager explained the seriousness of our mom's condition. We found out that our mom knew that nothing else could be done. Every organ was severely damaged and no treatment was possible. We cried as they explained to us that our mom was going to be transported to the hospice on Saturday when a bed would become available. After the fluid was removed my mom started to deteriorate right before our eyes. She was getting some words out but not like she was the day before. She asked for a candy bar even though she couldn't eat it. But to make her happy we gave her one. She just tasted it. She received all her requests. I don't know how God gave me the strength to handle this awful situation but he did.

On Saturday. I was nervous. I got dressed extra early and called my uncle to meet me at the hospice. I called my mom room prior to leaving to see what time they will be transporting her. My mom couldn't answer so I called the nurses station and asked the unit clerk if she could have my mom answered the phone. The secretary gave my mom the phone and she said "Hey, baby I love you. I love you. I love you. I love you. I love you. I love you". I said "Mom, I love you too and I will meet you at the hospice center."

At hospice my mom was surrounded by her loved ones throughout the day and close friends who came and prayed for her with us. Time went on and with me working as a certified nursing assistant for as long as I had, I knew that the end was near. My mom stopped talking and the visitors were slowly fading. I believed that this was all in God's plan because of the way it happened. It was like that Sunday when she called me. It was her and I. 10:15pm I heard the Smokie Norful song "I Need You Now" popped in my head and I posted it on social media for prayers because I needed it. I thought about the case manager telling my sisters and I that our mom was worried about us. I looked at my mom and said "Mom, I know you are tired and God knows you are tired too. So, I'm gonna promise you that my sisters and I will be ok. We will Mom. I promise. She placed her hands on her chest put her feet together and at 10:26, took 2 deep breaths and left. I kissed her forehead and told her I loved her.

5 months later, my nephew died. Accepting that was extremely hard. I couldn't grieve the way I needed for my mother or my nephew because I suddenly was dealing with a failed marriage. My mom prepared me to live without her. I know you might ask how. But she did she prepared me for the world. My mother taught me a lot of things growing up at a very young age. She taught me how to respect my elders, have manners, speak when spoken to, cook, do household chores, and never leave home without clean underwear on. My mom taught me how to fight my battles and look out for my sister. My mom left me with a lot of responsibilities, and she taught me how to cope.

CHAPTER 12
DADDY ISSUES

On February 14th 2019, I got a call from my cousin asking me why I didn't tell her my dad had cancer. I called my dad to find out why he didn't tell me. My dad did not want any of his children to know but he wanted us all at his upcoming doctor's appointment because they were going to discuss how long he had to live. Yet again, another devastating blow. My mom and now my dad feeling comfortable letting me know that they are dying soon. Some things that my dad expressed to me made sense but some things did not. It occurred to me my dad may have been experiencing the onset of dementia because of all the things he had been saying and doing did not make sense. I called everyone the day prior to the doctor's appointment and found out he never told his siblings or my siblings. We all went to his appointment. When meeting with the doctor she explained what type of cancer that my dad had and the expected prognosis. On top of living with sickle cell all his life he now had been diagnosed with multiple myeloma with amyloidosis. The doctor said he said 6 months to live but she wanted to send him to Jefferson Hospital for a 2nd opinion. My dad expressed to me what he wanted upon his death and I was strong enough to respect his wishes.

My dad was ok with dying. He also said that he didn't want me to worry so much. He had lived his life and to check his record. Again, I accepted all of this and promised myself I would hold on. I now knew with all that I've been thru that there was light at the end of the tunnel. Learning of my dad's illness, I put everything that I was mad at him aside and did all that he asked me to do. I did it because I do know that the Bible stated Honor your Mother and Father and your days will be long. Even though my dad hurt and disappointed me many times I loved him unconditionally.

FORGIVENESS

I miss my mom, I do but God knows the miles that she put on her body she needed to rest. I have a lot of unanswered questions that I just assumed the answers; because of what I later found out upon her death. Her father molested some of his daughters, the women he slept with, their daughters and even fathered children with them. My mom was 17 when her mother passed away and her father was still around then. So, my assumption is that he molested my mother and that is why she turned to drugs to suppress how she was feeling.

Forgiveness is something that I've struggled with for years. I was always enraged as teenager until adulthood because I felt everyone around me had a good life but me. I blamed my parents for my upbringing as difficult as it was. It was hard and I tried my best to be the best mom I can be to my son, and big sister to my sisters. I felt I was left to deal with tough responsibilities but I wouldn't change it for the world. It taught me to care love and cherish what I have. I forgave my mom for giving me responsibilities. I accepted that none of us are perfect. Forgiveness is a big deal because it helps you learn about yourself and your process. My mom put me out at the age of 17. I forgive her for that because I wouldn't be the woman I am. I forgive my mom for letting me have a baby I wasn't prepared for. I truly learned responsibility.

As for my dad, he was barely there for my sister and I. I forgive my dad for putting women before his children. I forgive him for never giving me the love I needed from a man. I forgive him for not walking me down the aisle at my wedding. I've learned that you have to forgive in order to move on. I had to forgive to grow. I actually felt better because I was the one hurting.

I am learning that forgiveness is for myself. I was struggling with forgiveness when it came to the end of my marriage because I did not expect this hurt that I experienced with what happened. I prayed to God to allow me to forgive my husband. I felt like I was robbed of my family that I had for the last 23 years and that was very painful. It is still a work in process and I am taking it day by day. I am thankful too I feel like a weight has been lifted from me. I feel like I am headed in the right direction. I can honestly thank my ex-husband for walking away because, look at me today.

CHAPTER 13
WOMEN ARE WINNING

I didn't like the number 23 after I ended my marriage!!!! I felt like 23 years was too much to let go. 23 years of memories, love, and family. It was painful to accept it was not an equal feeling of love and was a devastating blow. With my new mindset I embarked on a new and positive outlook of the number 23!

I realized that I was 23 when I met my ex-husband. The letter W is the 23rd letter of the alphabet. Which transcribes to me that women are winning. Today, we as women are claiming what's ours and recognizing are worth. 23 years in a relationship that served as a learning tool. I learned to deal with the ups and downs, life and death, building family, love and respect.

I looked up 23 in biblical terms. It took me to Psalms 23 and the part about "He leadeth me beside the still waters" stuck out to me. I believe it actually spoke to me (*Still waters are waters that flow very slowly and calmly; they bring much peace and rest to one's spirit*). One of the most relaxing things in life is the sound of a babbling brook or flowing stream of water. It is something that brings you to a place of calm, where you can focus without any distractions. In Hebrew, the words for 'still waters' in Psalm 23:2b are "Mai Menochot", meaning literally, "restful waters". Our Shepherd wants to lead us to a place of rest, a place of trust, a place of confidence, a place where you rely on Him and focus on Him without anything that will distract you. He wants to take the "heavy load" from your life and replace it with His everlasting peace and rest.

Then the Angel Number 23. Angel number 23 means that your guardian angels and the Ascended Masters are supporting you in your endeavors. Angels are messengers from the spiritual realm, carrying messages from Divine Source full of encouragement, inspiration, and optimism about your place in the universe. Level 23 was a metamorphosis for me! From the immature stage to the mature phase. I evolved. 23 is my genetic makeup of greatness. My children will be 23 and 32 this year. So, I say 23 was surely for me

It took me 23 years of not knowing my worth, not knowing who I was, not putting my wants, desires, and needs first to discover I deserved more. I don't have it all figured out. My story is still being written. I'm still learning, growing, and continuously striving for more.

I'm enjoying finally getting to know me. I'm enjoying putting myself first and finally I've learned how to love me.

TO BE CONTINUED.................

ABOUT THE AUTHOR

Growing up in the tough streets of Philadelphia, **Crystal Thomas** found herself a victim of her environment. With addiction all around; Thomas took on a woman role much earlier in life than she anticipated. Statistics continued as Thomas dropped out of school in the 8th grade. Shortly after she became a teenager mother. Accepting her now role, Thomas got comfortable with the system. With a change of events; Thomas started to want more. Thomas dropped the victim role and become the victor breaking all generational curses within her family. Thomas now has a Bachelor's Degree in Criminal Justice & Human Services, and is working towards her Master's. Thomas has 2 amazing sons whom she loves dearly and 2 precious grandchildren. Thomas mission is to inspire and assist women recovering from drugs and alcohol through her non-profit organization; **Diane's Way**. Thomas is in the process of opening **Diane's Way Recovery House** which will provide safe and affordable housing for women overcoming addiction

www.ingramcontent.com/pod-product-compliance
Lightning Source LLC
Chambersburg PA
CBHW070944160426
43194CB00030B/1951